GAO

Report to the Ranking Member, Committee on Homeland Security and Governmental Affairs, U.S. Senate

July 2012

TANF ELECTRONIC BENEFIT CARDS

Some States Are Restricting Certain TANF Transactions, but Challenges Remain

I0415789

G A O
Accountability * Integrity * Reliability

July 2012

GAO
Accountability * Integrity * Reliability
Highlights

Highlights of GAO-12-535, a report to the Ranking Member, Committee on Homeland Security and Governmental Affairs, U.S. Senate

TANF ELECTRONIC BENEFIT CARDS

Some States Are Restricting Certain TANF Transactions, but Challenges Remain

Why GAO Did This Study

The TANF block grant program provides federal grants to states for various benefits and activities, including cash welfare for needy families with children. TANF is overseen at the federal level by HHS, and administered by states. Most states disburse TANF cash assistance through electronic benefit cards, which can be used to withdraw money or make purchases. Media coverage highlighted cases of cardholders accessing benefits at casinos and other locations that were considered inconsistent with the purpose of TANF. In February 2012, Congress passed a law requiring states to prevent certain transactions at casinos, liquor stores, and adult-entertainment establishments. Within 2 years of enactment, the law also requires HHS to oversee states' compliance with these requirements.

GAO was asked to review the ability of TANF recipients to withdraw TANF funds at certain locations inconsistent with the purpose of TANF, such as gambling or other establishments. To do so, GAO reviewed documentation and interviewed officials from HHS, key industry stakeholders, and the top 10 states in TANF basic block grant dollars. GAO also assessed the completeness and accuracy of EBT transaction data from federal fiscal year 2010 from 4 of the 10 states selected. GAO selected these 4 states on the basis of geographical diversity, and the results of this data analysis cannot be generalized to other states.

What GAO Recommends

GAO is not making any recommendations.

View GAO-12-535. For more information, contact Gregory D. Kutz at (202) 512-6722 or kutzg@gao.gov.

What GAO Found

Six of the 10 states reviewed by GAO took steps aimed at preventing certain Temporary Assistance for Needy Families (TANF) transactions determined to be inconsistent with the purpose of TANF, despite no federal requirement to do so at the time. Restrictions are based on selected states' laws, executive orders, and other regulations, and generally cover certain locations or certain types of purchases such as alcohol. In some cases, states' restrictions are broader than the new federal requirements. These restrictions vary in their degree and means of implementation, including widespread disabling of Electronic Benefit Transfer (EBT) access at automated teller machines located at certain locations across a state, such as at casinos. The other 4 states had no restrictions because no laws, executive orders, or other regulations prohibited certain transactions based on the location of the transactions or the nature of the goods or services purchased. These states did not implement restrictions due to concerns about cost-effectiveness or technical limitations, according to state officials.

Challenges experienced by states in implementing their current restrictions could inhibit future restriction efforts, including those intended to address new federal requirements. These challenges included difficulties with identifying certain locations that could be prohibited and limitations in available data. For example, the transaction data states receive do not contain information that is accurate or detailed enough for them to identify locations that can potentially be prohibited or restricted. State officials suggested that improvements in the completeness and accuracy of transaction data might better enable them to prevent such transactions. In its assessment of the EBT transaction data from 4 states, GAO found that the data are insufficient for systematic monitoring. To effectively conduct systematic monitoring, including the identification of locations that could be blocked from TANF access, data should be complete and accurate. However, addressing the limitations that GAO found in the transaction data—such as requiring accurate merchant category codes for retailers—could involve significant resources. States that prohibit certain types of purchases generally do not have ways to track what items recipients buy with their cards, partially due to the lack of information in transaction data on specific goods or services purchased. States were also challenged in attempting to track the spending of cash withdrawn with cards. With no controls on how or where individuals spend withdrawn cash, a recipient could withdraw money at an authorized location and use it at certain locations or for certain purchases restricted by some states.

As of July 2012, the Department of Health and Human Services (HHS) was at the beginning of its rulemaking process and did not yet know what form its regulations would take. Until HHS issues regulations or provides further guidance as to what policies and practices are sufficient to comply with new federal requirements, it is unclear to what extent the various restrictions implemented by states would be in compliance. States' restrictions could help inform HHS's oversight efforts, especially any information on the cost-effectiveness and success rates for various state restrictions. Restriction methods that do not rely on flawed transaction data may be the most practical.

We provided HHS with a draft of our report for comment. HHS stated that our report's findings and analysis will be helpful as it drafts implementing regulations, and it provided technical comments that we incorporated, as appropriate.

_____

__United States Government Accountability Office__

Contents

Abbreviations

AFDC	Aid to Families with Dependent Children
ATM	automated teller machine
BIN	bank identification number
CDSS	California Department of Social Services
DSHS	Washington State Department of Social and Health Services
EBT	Electronic Benefit Transfer
EPC	electronic payment card
FNS	Food and Nutrition Service
HHS	Department of Health and Human Services
HHSC	Texas Health and Human Services Commission
MOE	maintenance of effort
OSI	California Office of Systems Integration
POS	point-of-sale
PRWORA	Personal Responsibility and Work Opportunity Reconciliation Act of 1996
SNAP	Supplemental Nutrition Assistance Program
TANF	Temporary Assistance for Needy Families
TIGER	Topologically Integrated Geographic Encoding and Referencing
USDA	Department of Agriculture

United States Government Accountability Office
Washington, DC 20548

July 20, 2012

The Honorable Susan M. Collins
Ranking Member
Committee on Homeland Security and Governmental Affairs
United States Senate

Dear Senator Collins:

The Department of Health and Human Services (HHS) oversees states' administration of the Temporary Assistance to Needy Families (TANF) program to provide cash assistance, childcare, and other services to low-income families. Among the program's goals are the promotion of job preparation, employment, and marriage among parents of dependent children. HHS oversees the program at the federal level and distributes $16.5 billion in annual federal block grants to states to provide benefits and services to recipients. As a federal block-grant program, TANF allows states broad flexibility in designing and implementing their programs. To purchase goods and services, TANF recipients receive cash assistance, which in most states they can access at automated teller machines (ATM), banks, or retailers, using Electronic Benefit Transfer (EBT) cards. Cash assistance may be used for goods and services, and the amount of cash assistance received can vary by state.[1] The EBT cards are similar to debit or stored-value cards, but do not carry a line of credit, and the purchases or withdrawals made with these cards cannot exceed the amount of recipients' TANF benefits as determined by each state's TANF program.

Until February 2012, there were no nationwide federal requirements for states to take steps aimed at preventing access to TANF cash assistance at certain locations. However, media coverage in some states highlighted cases of individuals accessing cash or conducting transactions at gambling establishments, adult-entertainment establishments, and liquor stores that could be considered inconsistent with the TANF program. In response, some states took steps aimed at implementing certain

---

[1] TANF cash benefits are set by states. In July 2010, the maximum monthly benefit for a family of three ranged from $923 in Alaska to $170 in Mississippi. Benefits in all states represent a fraction of poverty-level income. In the median jurisdiction (Kansas), the maximum monthly benefit was $429 for a family of three.

GAO-12-535 TANF Electronic Benefit Cards

restrictions that would prevent such transactions. In February 2012, Congress passed, as part of the Middle Class Tax Relief and Job Creation Act of 2012, the Welfare Integrity and Data Improvement Act, which requires all states to maintain policies and practices as necessary to prevent TANF assistance from being used in any electronic benefit transfer transaction in (1) liquor stores; (2) casinos, gambling casinos, or gaming establishments; and (3) adult-oriented entertainment establishments in which performers disrobe or perform in an unclothed state for entertainment.[2] States must report to HHS the steps they have taken to implement such policies and practices by February 22, 2014.

In this context, you asked us to review the ability of TANF recipients to withdraw TANF funds at certain locations inconsistent with the purpose of TANF, such as gambling or other establishments. To understand this ability better, we reviewed actions selected states have taken to prevent unauthorized TANF transactions, and the challenges they can face in taking such steps in compliance with new federal legislation.[3] To perform our work, we reviewed TANF laws, regulations, and other documentation and interviewed officials from HHS. We also reviewed documentation and interviewed officials from the top 10 states in terms of TANF basic block-grant dollars—California, New York, Michigan, Ohio, Pennsylvania, Illinois, Florida, Texas, Massachusetts, and Washington. These 10 states received the greatest TANF basic block-grant dollars, and collectively represent 66 percent of the TANF basic block grants funded in federal fiscal year 2012. In addition, we interviewed and reviewed documentation from key industry stakeholders, including EBT vendors, related to the selected states' efforts to prevent unauthorized TANF transactions.

We also obtained EBT card-transaction data from 4 of the 10 selected states—California, Florida, New York, and Texas—covering transactions from federal fiscal year 2010.[4] We selected these 4 states on the basis of geographical diversity. The results of our analysis of these 4 states' data cannot be generalized to other states. Using these data, we assessed the extent to which the data would allow the 4 selected states to conduct systematic monitoring to identify unauthorized transactions. To do so, we

---

[2]Pub. L. No. 112–96, § 4004, 126 Stat. 156, 197 - 198.

[3]For the purposes of this report, we consider "unauthorized" to mean all TANF transactions that are prohibited under state laws, regulations, policies, or other actions.

[4]October 1, 2009, to September 30, 2010.

used a generalizable, random sample of each of the 4 selected states' EBT transaction data[5] and compared it to electronic geo-coding information that pinpoints places and identifies locations.[6] We also assessed whether the data would allow the 4 selected states to identify individual TANF transactions at certain types of locations by conducting keyword searches of merchant names for terms associated with casinos, liquor stores, and adult-entertainment establishments. We conducted electronic data testing to determine the reliability of the California, Florida, New York, and Texas EBT data. For all four states, we determined that the EBT data are not sufficiently reliable for the purpose of performing systematic monitoring of transactions in locations that are inconsistent with the purposes of TANF. However, EBT transaction data are sufficiently reliable for the purpose of identifying examples of transactions with merchant names that contain words associated with casinos, liquor stores, and adult-entertainment establishments. A more-detailed description of our scope and methodology is provided in appendix I.

We conducted this performance audit from October 2011 to July 2012 in accordance with generally accepted government auditing standards. Those standards require that we plan and perform the audit to obtain sufficient, appropriate evidence to provide a reasonable basis for our findings and conclusions based on our audit objectives. We believe that the evidence obtained provides a reasonable basis for our findings and conclusions based on our audit objectives.

---

[5]The random samples can only generalize about each state using each state's sample, not about other states and not nationally. For example, the Texas sample tells us something general about the Texas EBT data as a whole, but cannot tell us anything about the California data or all EBT transaction data nationally.

[6]We compared EBT transaction addresses to U.S. Census Bureau's Topologically Integrated Geographic Encoding and Referencing (TIGER) standard addresses.

Background

TANF Funding and Program Goals

The Personal Responsibility and Work Opportunity Reconciliation Act of 1996 (PRWORA)[7] significantly changed federal welfare policy for low-income families with children, from a program that entitled eligible families to monthly cash payments to a capped block grant that emphasizes employment and work supports for most adult recipients. As part of PRWORA, Congress created the TANF program,[8] through which HHS provides states about $16.5 billion each year in block grant funds to implement the program. To receive the TANF block grant, each state must also spend at least a specified level of its own funds, which is referred to as state maintenance of effort (MOE).[9] In creating the TANF block grant, PRWORA defines four goals for the program:

1. provide assistance so that children could be cared for in their own homes or in the homes of relatives;
2. end families' dependence on government benefits by promoting job preparation, work, and marriage;
3. prevent and reduce the incidence of out-of-wedlock pregnancies; and
4. encourage the formation and maintenance of two-parent families.

TANF is a flexible funding stream that states can use to provide cash assistance and a wide range of services that are "reasonably calculated" to further the program's four goals.[10] In federal fiscal year 2011, states used about 29 percent of their TANF funds on basic assistance that included cash assistance for needy families,[11] and the remaining funds were spent on other purposes, such as child care, employment programs,

---

[7]Pub. L. No. 104-193, 110 Stat. 2105.

[8]TANF replaced the Aid to Families with Dependent Children (AFDC) program. Id. § 103(a)(1), 110 Stat. 2105, 2112.

[9]42 U.S.C. § 609(a)(7); 45 C.F.R. §§ 263.1 – 263.9. To meet the MOE requirement, each state must generally spend 75 or 80 percent of what it spent in fiscal year 1994 on welfare-related programs, including AFDC, Job Opportunities and Basic Skills Training, Emergency Assistance, and AFDC-related child-care programs.

[10]42 U.S.C. § 604(a).

[11]Throughout this report, we refer to families receiving TANF cash assistance, for ease of reporting. However, this is a simplification of PRWORA, which actually refers to families receiving "assistance." 42 U.S.C. § 603.

and child welfare services.[12] Due to the flexibility given to states, TANF programs differ substantially by state. States are required to develop plans that outline their intended use of funds and report data on families receiving assistance. While the federal TANF statute does not define "assistance," HHS defines assistance in regulation as cash payments, vouchers, and other forms of benefits designed to meet a family's "ongoing basic needs," such as food, clothing, shelter, utilities, household goods, personal-care items, and general incidental expenses.[13]

TANF Cash Assistance Disbursement Methods

Traditionally, states disbursed cash assistance benefit payments by means of paper check. The EBT program was devised in the 1980s originally to meet the needs of the Department of Agriculture's (USDA) Food Stamp Program, in which federal benefits were electronically disbursed to eligible recipients. These cards are not tied to a consumer asset account, and generally the account structures and processing requirements differ from other payment cards. EBT cards can be used to deliver benefits to banked and unbanked recipients and can be used to deliver multiple benefits using a single card. The cost savings in the Food Stamp Program (now known as the Supplemental Nutrition Assistance Program or SNAP) from using electronic payments to distribute benefits prompted states to use EBT cards to also distribute TANF benefits electronically, leveraging the existent EBT system designed for SNAP. Electronic benefit distribution methods also include Electronic Payment Cards (EPC). Some EPC cards are prepaid or debit cards that are branded with a MasterCard, American Express, Discover, or Visa logo, which allows cardholders to conduct signature-based transactions anywhere that those brands are accepted as well as at ATM and point-of-sale (POS) machines.

Electronic benefit cards—both EBT and EPC—generally can be used like traditional debit or credit cards, in that recipients can use them at ATMs to withdraw cash, or at retailers' POS terminals for purchases or to receive cash by selecting a cash-back option. However, there are some key differences between the electronic benefit card and commercial credit

---

[12]States may use TANF funds to support a variety of child welfare services, such as screening for child abuse and neglect, case-management activities, and cash assistance and services for relative caregivers.

[13]45 C.F.R. § 260.31.

cards. The main difference is that electronic benefit cards do not carry a credit line, and the purchases or withdrawals made with these cards cannot exceed the amount of recipients' TANF benefits. With commercial credit cards, cardholders borrow to make a purchase and then pay the money back later. Electronic benefit cards are more like debit or stored-value cards and provide an alternative to cash—each time that a cardholder uses his or her electronic benefit card, the money spent or withdrawn is deducted from the cardholder's TANF benefits account.

States consider various factors when implementing EBT or EPC programs, including potential financial burden to recipients, such as transaction fees at ATMs that charge a surcharge for each transaction; recipient characteristics, such as disabilities; implementation costs; and fraud and security risks. States also take into account how readily recipients can access cash assistance. For example, in some rural areas or low-income neighborhoods the only access point for cash assistance benefits may be a location such as a grocery store, single depository institution, or even a liquor store. Some of the benefits to recipients from states choosing EBT or EPC programs include quicker disbursement of benefits, the elimination of lost or undelivered paper checks, access to benefits without an established bank account, and no need to locate check-cashing venues in order to access benefits.

Recent TANF Legislative Changes

Prior to 2012, states were not required under federal law to take steps aimed at preventing specific TANF transactions at certain locations. However, the Welfare Integrity and Data Improvement Act, part of the Middle Class Tax Relief and Job Creation Act of 2012, signed into law on February 22, 2012, introduced several changes to TANF that can affect recipients' ability to access cash assistance at certain locations.[14] Specifically, the Act requires that each state receiving a TANF block grant

---

[14]Pub. L. No. 112–96, § 4004, 126 Stat. 156, 197 - 198.

maintain policies and practices as necessary to prevent TANF assistance from being used in any "electronic benefit transfer transaction"[15] in

- any liquor store;[16]
- any casino, gambling casino, or gaming establishment;[17] or
- any retail establishment that provides adult-oriented entertainment in which performers disrobe or perform in an unclothed state for entertainment.

The Act calls for HHS to determine whether states have implemented and maintained policies and practices to prevent such transactions, within 2 years of the Act's enactment. If HHS determines that a state has not implemented and maintained these policies and practices, or if a state has not reported to HHS on its policies and practices, HHS may reduce the state's family assistance grant by an amount equal to 5 percent of the state's grant amount for the federal fiscal year following the 2-year period after enactment and each succeeding federal fiscal year in which the state does not demonstrate that it has implemented and maintained such policies and practices. However, HHS may reduce the amount of this penalty on the basis of the degree of noncompliance of the state in question. In addition, the Act specifies that states are not responsible for individuals who engage in fraudulent activity to circumvent the state's policies and practices, and will not face a reduction in their family assistance grant amounts in such cases.[18]

---

[15]The Act defines electronic benefit transfer transaction as "the use of a credit or debit card service, automated teller machine, point-of-sale terminal, or access to an online system for the withdrawal of funds or the processing of a payment for merchandise or a service." Id. § 4004(a), 126 Stat. 197.

[16]The Act defines liquor store as "any retail establishment which sells exclusively or primarily intoxicating liquor. Such term does not include a grocery store which sells both intoxicating liquor and groceries including staple foods (within the meaning of section 3(r) of the Food and Nutrition Act of 2008 (7 U.S.C. 2012(r)))." Id.

[17]The Act states that the terms casino, gambling casino, and gaming establishment do not include "(I) a grocery store which sells groceries including such staple foods and which also offers, or is located within the same building or complex as, casino, gambling, or gaming activities; or (II) any other establishment that offers casino, gambling, or gaming activities incidental to the principal purpose of the business." Id.

[18]Id., § 4004(b), 126 Stat. 197 - 198.

The Act also contains requirements for states related to maintaining recipients' access to TANF cash assistance. As part of the plan that each state is required to submit to HHS,[19] states must include policies and procedures to ensure that recipients have adequate access to their cash assistance. In addition, states must ensure that recipients have access to using or withdrawing assistance with minimal fees or charges, including an opportunity to access assistance with no fees or charges, and that they are provided information on applicable fees and surcharges that apply to electronic fund transactions involving the assistance, and that such information is made publicly available.[20]

HHS issued a request for public comment in April 2012, seeking information by June 2012 on: how states deliver TANF assistance to beneficiaries, whether states have implemented policies and practices to prevent electronic benefit transfer transactions at the locations mentioned above, states' experiences with these policies and practices, and other similar restrictions states place on TANF assistance usage.[21] In its notice, HHS identified multiple questions for states to answer, including questions on the methods states use to track the locations where transactions occur, challenges states experienced when implementing any restrictions on transactions at certain locations, the initial and ongoing costs of restrictions, the effectiveness of restrictions and the factors influencing the effectiveness, and any concerns that have been raised about the restrictions, among other things. In addition, HHS requested input from states' EBT vendors on potential issues that states may face in implementing restrictions, including technical issues, cost implications, access implications, and mechanisms for addressing problems identified.

---

[19]42 U.S.C. § 602(a).

[20]Pub. L. No. 112–96, § 4004(c), 126 Stat. 156, 198.

[21]77 Fed. Reg. 24667 (Apr. 25, 2012).

Some States Are Restricting Certain TANF Transactions, but Face Challenges Because of Data Limitations and Other Factors

Six of the 10 states we reviewed have taken steps to prevent certain types of inappropriate TANF transactions—restrictions that in some cases are broader than recent federal requirements that require states to take steps aimed at preventing transactions in casinos, liquor stores, and adult-entertainment establishments. These 6 states faced a variety of challenges in identifying inappropriate locations and preventing transactions at these locations. At the time these efforts were undertaken, there were no federal requirements that required states to take steps aimed at restricting such transactions. In addition, EBT transaction data from federal fiscal year 2010 from 4 of the 10 selected states were generally incomplete or unreliable, and were of limited use to the states for systematically identifying or monitoring inappropriate locations. While the federal requirements to restrict inappropriate transactions now exist, data issues and other challenges, if unaddressed, may continue to affect efforts to comply with these new requirements.

Some States Have Attempted to Restrict TANF Transactions

Six of the 10 states we selected and reviewed have taken steps to prevent certain types of TANF transactions; these actions vary in their degree and means of implementation, from widespread disabling of EBT access at ATMs in certain locations across a state to, according to officials from one state, passing a law without implementing steps for enforcing it. The restrictions generally involve prohibiting the use of EBT cards at certain locations or prohibiting purchases of certain goods or services, or both, as shown in figure 1 below. In 4 of the 10 selected states, there were no restrictions on TANF transactions, as no transactions were unauthorized based on the location of the transactions or the nature of the goods or services purchased. As mentioned above, before the 2012 enactment of federal legislation, states were not required by the federal government to maintain or implement policies and practices aimed at preventing TANF transactions based on the location of the transactions. Figure 1 below, an interactive map, provides rollover information (see interactive instructions below) that describes the steps that selected states have taken aimed at preventing the use of TANF cash assistance for certain purchases or in certain locations. (See app. II for the steps taken within each selected state.)

Figure 1: Some States Have Taken Steps Aimed at Preventing Unauthorized TANF Transactions

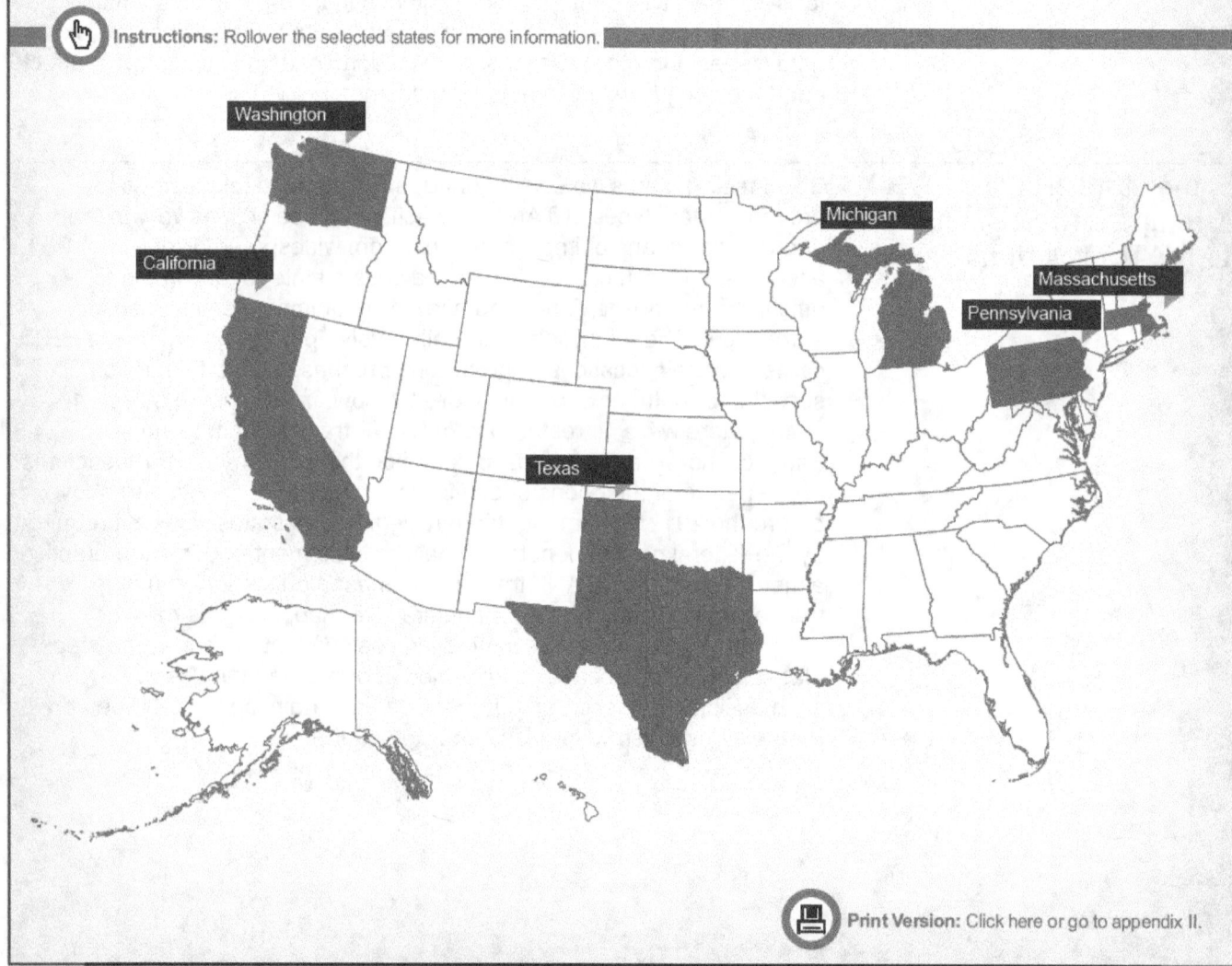

Source: GAO (data); Map Resources (map).

Some of the selected states experienced various challenges while attempting to prevent certain TANF transactions. Some states' restriction activities were impeded by transaction data that did not allow them to identify sufficiently or monitor locations that were prohibited in their state. In some cases, states have attempted to address these challenges through ongoing monitoring and other efforts. In addition, some of the selected states' restrictions currently lack means of enforcement. For example, some states that prohibit certain types of purchases generally do not have ways to track what items recipients buy with their cash assistance, partially due to the lack of information in transaction data on what items are bought with EBT cards. There are also challenges for states in attempting to track cash spending. With no controls on how or where individuals spend their cash benefits, a recipient could withdraw money at an authorized location and then use it at certain locations or for certain purchases restricted by some states.

States with Restrictions

California

In response to media attention, and a California executive order, California's Department of Social Services (CDSS) and its EBT vendor took steps to disable TANF access at thousands of ATMs; however, they have faced certain technical and legal limitations. In June 2010, the Governor of California issued an executive order requiring that CDSS prevent TANF recipients from accessing their benefits at ATMs in gambling establishments.[22] The executive order resulted from news reports that revealed that state TANF recipients had accessed their benefits at ATMs located in gambling establishments. The order stated that benefits are provided to pay for the families' basic subsistence needs and not for gambling. From June 2010 to December 2010, and pursuant to this executive order, CDSS issued notices explaining its intent to expand the number of locations where EBT access to TANF cash assistance would be eliminated. This effort required disabling EBT access at ATMs in locations that fall under at least 14 different prohibited categories (see fig. 1 above).

Officials from CDSS and the state's Office of Systems Integration (OSI) worked with the state's EBT vendor and other parties to identify and block these locations from EBT access. For example, CDSS officials stated that

---

[22]Cal. Exec. Ord. S-09-10 (June 24, 2010).

CDSS approached California's casino commission, requesting that it notify CDSS if it found EBT cards being used within licensed California casinos. In addition, CDSS officials stated that they reached out to the California Office of Alcoholic Beverage Control in order to determine, identify, and deactivate liquor stores that were not already authorized by the Food and Nutrition Service (FNS), which oversees the Supplemental Nutrition Assistance Program (SNAP). To identify and block additional locations, CDSS and OSI officials manually searched EBT transaction records for business names that appeared to belong to one of the prohibited categories. For example, OSI searched for terms such as "beer," "wine," "spirit," "tattoo," "piercing," and other words that related to the prohibited categories. In addition, OSI used lists of tribal casinos and card rooms located in the state and corresponding addresses to verify against the EBT transaction data. After identifying potential locations to be blocked, officials performed Internet searches to attempt to verify the type of location. However, California officials noted that the accuracy of Internet searches cannot be validated because it is not clear whether the information on the Internet is current. For example, when looking at satellite photos of streets on the Internet to verify a restricted location, the Internet photo may show a vacant building or building under construction because the photo could be 1 to 2 years old, according to California officials.

Once officials confirmed that the businesses appeared to belong in one of the 14 prohibited categories, then they provided the state's EBT vendor with locations that needed to be blocked. The vendor contacted the responsible third-party processor to request that the ATMs at these locations be disabled from accepting the state's EBT card. To do so, the processors deactivated the state's bank identification number (BIN) at each terminal. CDSS and OSI provided the state's Department of Justice with nonloaded EBT cards so that it could test ATMs at gambling establishments to determine whether they are in compliance.

According to CDSS officials, as of February 2012, EBT access was disabled at approximately 6,328 ATMs in California, out of a total of approximately 35,400 ATMs in California that have performed EBT transactions. However, state officials noted that they experienced challenges with identifying locations to block. For example, according to state officials, the EBT transaction data contain incomplete or inaccurate fields, including key information on the location of transactions. California officials said that the EBT transaction data sometimes contain misspelled addresses, and do not provide information on what type of retailers were involved for each transaction. In addition, California officials told us that the address information included in the EBT transaction data is sometimes that of retailers' corporate offices rather than the location where the transactions actually took place. State officials said that there is no code available in the EBT transaction data that would allow them to identify easily the nature of each retailer.[23] While their EBT vendor receives merchant category codes for some ATM transactions, this information has limitations because a known issue is that some ATMs have the same merchant category code that identifies the location of the transaction as a financial institution rather than any categories associated with the particular nature of the business where the transaction occurred. To work around the limitations in the EBT transaction data, California officials told us that their staff conducted online research to verify whether businesses actually fell under one of the state's prohibited categories. However, they said that this was a manual, time-intensive process that involved making judgments about the nature of retailers, which can be subjective and prone to error. According to California officials, some ATMs at liquor stores were reactivated because they were initially identified as liquor stores not authorized by the U.S. Department of Agriculture's Food and Nutrition Service (FNS),[24] but others were reactivated because the storeowner applied for FNS authorization after having the ATM deactivated. In those stores, the ATM was reactivated as the new FNS authorization was verified.

California officials told us that their EBT vendor also conducts ongoing monitoring of transaction data to identify terminals blocked formerly that then change location or are reactivated, as well as transactions at new locations with names that appear to fall under one of the state's prohibited categories. State officials also told us that the transaction data only allow them to identify locations where transactions have already occurred, so they are unable to assess the universe of locations that might fall under prohibited categories. For example, although they disabled EBT access at thousands of ATMs that have performed EBT transactions, as mentioned

---

[23]As discussed below, we identified limitations in the accuracy and completeness of the transaction data from four states. In addition, officials from multiple states expressed concerns about the data similar to our findings and the views of California officials.

[24]Any retailer that would like to allow its customers to use their federal food benefits from the Supplemental Nutrition Assistance Program (SNAP) must be authorized by FNS to participate in SNAP. According to FNS, the only form of SNAP benefit issuance is the EBT card. EBT allows the retailer, such as a liquor store, to accept SNAP payment for food using the EBT card.

above, officials said that there are likely many more ATMs that exist in the state, but they cannot be identified until a transaction takes place there. As a result, CDSS is unable to use the EBT transaction data and its methodology noted above to identify all ATMs in California locations that may fall under the 14 prohibited categories.

In addition, although CDSS has expressed its intent to disable TANF access at POS devices that fall under the 14 categories, officials from CDSS and the state's EBT vendor told us that they have been unable to disable EBT access at any POS terminals as of March 2012. CDSS officials stated that POS terminals will be blocked sometime in the future, but they did not know when this would occur because third-party processors are finding it difficult to block POS terminals as opposed to ATMs. For example, according to CDSS's vendor, identification numbers for POS terminals are generally not as unique as those assigned to ATMs. Specifically, POS terminals located in many retailers in California and across the country use the same terminal identification numbers as opposed to unique terminal identification numbers, which may result in third-party processors accidentally blocking POS terminals at locations that were not intended to be blocked, including some that are located outside of California.

Further, it is not illegal under California state law for a California resident to use his or her EBT card at one of the prohibited locations. In fact, California state law still includes a provision that specifically protects the rights of individuals to spend their cash assistance as they want in California. The California statute states, "[n]o person concerned with the administration of a public assistance program shall dictate how any recipient shall expend the aid granted to him."[25] Implementing this statute, CDSS's Manual of Policies and Procedures: Eligibility and Assistance Standards states "[e]ach individual or family has the right to manage his/her own affairs; to decide what use of his/her money, including the aid payment, will best serve his/her interests."[26] Such broad treatment, while consistent with California state law, raises questions about the extent to which California's current controls will help to ensure that cash assistance is being used in a manner consistent with the purposes of the TANF program and the new federal requirements. Until HHS issues regulations

---

[25]Cal. Welf. & Inst. Code § 10501.

[26]Cal. Dep't. Soc. Serv. Manual Pol'y. & Proc. § 44-301.

or provides further guidance as to what policies and practices are sufficient to comply with the new federal requirements, it is unclear whether there is any conflict between the new federal law and California's statute.

Massachusetts

Although Massachusetts has made certain TANF transactions illegal, the state has not yet finalized plans for enforcing its legal restrictions and has not blocked any transactions. Specifically, state TANF officials have not yet taken steps aimed at enforcing the legal restrictions or monitoring compliance. As of July 2011, Massachusetts state law prohibits individuals from using their cash assistance to purchase alcohol, tobacco, and lottery tickets.[27] Individuals who make a purchase in violation of the law are required to reimburse the state for the purchase, and are also banned from receiving benefits for varying periods, according to state law.[28] The law also states that individuals or store owners who knowingly accept direct cash assistance funds held on EBT cards for the purchase of alcoholic beverages, lottery tickets, or tobacco products will be fined not more than $500 for the first offense, not less than $500 or more than $1,000 for the second offense, and not less than $1,000 for the third or subsequent offense.[29] However, as of July 2012, Massachusetts had not yet finalized plans for enforcing the law and had not blocked any transactions. State officials told us that they are unable to track or identify the types of items or services recipients actually purchase with the TANF cash assistance withdrawn using their EBT cards at ATMs or POS terminals. For example, according to state officials, EBT transaction data do not contain information on what items are purchased using EBT cards. According to a Massachusetts official, the state has not yet blocked any purchases because it does not have the manual or technological processes to do so.

In December 2011, Massachusetts law also mandated the creation of an EBT Commission to study and report on, among other things, the use of EBT cards for the purchase of products such as firearms, tobacco, lottery

---

[27]Mass. Gen. Laws ch. 18, § 5I.

[28]Id.

[29]Mass. Gen. Laws ch. 18, § 5J.

tickets, and alcohol.[30] The commission was tasked with developing recommendations for the state legislature, including recommendations on how to prevent the inappropriate use of EBT cards. The commission met between February and March 2012 and determined that EBT transaction data do not capture information on what items are purchased with EBT cards, which makes blocking specific items from being purchased with an EBT card impossible technologically. In compliance with, and in addition to implementing the new federal law, the commission recommended and stated that legislative members of the commission will file legislation in Massachusetts that will ban EBT transactions at ATMs and POS terminals in liquor stores, casinos and gaming establishments, adult-oriented entertainment establishments, nail salons, tattoo parlors, firearms dealers, bars/drinking establishments, smoke shops, and spas. The commission discussed, but did not recommend, implementing further restrictions on recipients' use of cash. For example, the commission considered, but chose not to recommend, limiting the amount of cash assistance that can be withdrawn from ATMs or POS terminals either entirely or to 50 percent of each recipient's monthly cash benefit amount. However, the commission determined that restricting cash access this way could incentivize fraud and trafficking of EBT cards. In addition, the commission did not want to cause additional hardship for recipients who use their cash assistance appropriately to pay for rent, transportation, and other essential costs. Moreover, the commission learned that its EBT vendor did not have current functionality to restrict each recipient's cash access at ATMs to only 50 percent of his or her total monthly benefit amount.

Michigan

Michigan has a procedure in place that prohibits certain uses of TANF cash assistance, but does not have a way to track whether recipients adhere to state requirements. Beginning in October 2011, Michigan law required that TANF recipients' family self-sufficiency plans—which families must execute in return for receiving assistance—must include a prohibition on using assistance to purchase lottery tickets, alcohol, or tobacco, or for gambling, illegal activities or other nonessential items.[31] If a recipient does not adhere to the requirements of his or her family self-

---

[30]2011 Mass. Acts ch. 219.

[31]Mich. Comp. Laws § 400.57e.

sufficiency plan, the state can impose penalties based on the number of instances of noncompliance. For example, the third instance of noncompliance can result in the family being permanently ineligible from receiving program assistance.[32] In addition to the prohibited items or activities noted above, state policy also bars recipients from using cash assistance for adult entertainment, massage parlors, spas, tattoo shops, bail bond agencies, and cruise ships.[33] However, state officials told us that they do not have any way to track how recipients spend cash withdrawn with EBT cards, and that EBT card data do not include information on what purchases recipients make with their cards.

In addition, in a letter sent to Michigan casinos in 2011, the state governor's office expressed its decision to correct flaws in Michigan's EBT card program, and tighten the rules for Michigan's EBT card use by prohibiting clients from using their EBT card to withdraw cash from any ATM machine located in any casino in Michigan, due to reports of possible abuse committed by some of Michigan's TANF recipients. As a result, state officials said that Michigan casinos contacted third-party processors and financial institutions to ask that they block the state's BIN at ATMs located in the casinos, thereby cutting off EBT access there. State officials told us that they later had the state's EBT vendor conduct a query to determine whether transactions were still occurring at casinos. The vendor ran six separate queries, but identified no EBT transactions at casinos after the EBT access was disabled, including one casino where state officials said that they had previously identified $87,340 in EBT transactions. State officials said that ATMs have not been blocked yet at locations other than casinos. In addition, EBT access at POS terminals has not yet been disabled at restricted locations, and state officials are unaware of EBT access being disabled at POS terminals in Michigan casinos. Michigan officials noted that EBT vendors do not have a suitable electronic method of disabling the use of EBT cards in certain types of businesses, whether at POS devices or at ATMs. Michigan officials noted two contributing problems with identifying locations and disabling EBT access at certain locations. First, identifying the type of location is dependent on the business accurately reporting data on the nature of its business, according to Michigan officials. Second, although the banking and ATM industries are the entities that collect the business type and

---

[32]Mich. Comp. Laws § 400.57g.

[33]Michigan Bridges Eligibility Manual (BPB 2011-023) §§ 228, 230A, and 515.

GAO-12-535 TANF Electronic Benefit Cards

location data, and they have the means to disable access at any location, they have not been mandated to assist the states in this effort.

Pennsylvania

Pennsylvania prevents EBT use at state-run liquor stores and obtained the cooperation of casinos in disabling EBT access on their premises. In addition, since December 2009, it has been illegal under Pennsylvania state law to purchase liquor or alcohol with an electronic benefits card.[34] Under Pennsylvania law, a person found to violate knowingly this law shall be guilty of a misdemeanor, and, upon conviction, shall be sentenced to pay a fine, not exceeding $100, or to undergo imprisonment, not exceeding 6 months, or both.[35] Liquor stores in Pennsylvania are operated by the state. According to state officials, these liquor stores do not accept the state's EBT card at POS devices, and there are no ATMs in these state-run liquor stores. In response to bills introduced, but not passed, in the state assembly that would have prohibited EBT access at casinos,[36] state officials from the gaming control commission contacted a third-party processor for ATMs at casinos to ask the processor to deactivate the state's bank identification number (BIN) from those machines. State officials told us that they assessed the effectiveness of the restrictions by sending staff members with working EBT cards to three casinos to check in person whether the casinos' ATMs accepted EBT cards. Although some of the ATMs still accepted EBT cards at first, state officials told us that those machines were eventually blocked from accepting further EBT transactions. According to Pennsylvania officials, when they conducted pilot monitoring of their restrictions, they had to look up retailer information on the Internet because the transaction data did not contain information that allowed them to determine what type of businesses the retailers were.

Texas

As opposed to restricting categories of locations that had previously accepted TANF EBT cards, the design of Texas's TANF program places

---

[34] 62 Pa. Cons. Stat. § 484.

[35] 62 Pa. Cons. Stat. § 483.

[36] Pa. S.B. 975 (2011) and Pa. H.B. 1254 (2011).

limitations on the participation in the state EBT network of retailers that derive most of their revenue from alcohol, gambling, adult entertainment, and other functions. Since the mid-1990s, Texas has required that retailers seeking to participate in the state's EBT system must be: (1) authorized by FNS to provide food services to SNAP recipients; or (2) a non-FNS authorized retailer that receives no more than 10 percent of its gross revenue from entertainment, such as from the sale of alcoholic beverages, legalized games of chance, sexually oriented materials, coin-operated amusement machines or amusement services.[37] According to officials with the state's Health and Human Services Commission (HHSC), third-party processors are responsible for ensuring that retailers comply with these requirements. In addition, state officials said that third-party processors send them a list of TANF-only retailers,[38] which HHSC uses to monitor locations that appear to be in noncompliance on the basis of the retailers' names. State officials added that they implemented a more-rigorous monitoring process in 2011, but were not aware of any retailers removed from the EBT program for noncompliance.

Since September 1997, a Texas state statute has required that recipients use TANF benefits to purchase only goods and services necessary and essential to the welfare of the family, such as food, clothing, housing, utilities, child care, transportation, and medicine, medical supplies, or equipment not covered by Medicaid.[39] State officials told us that they are unable to track how recipients spend their cash assistance. However, they said that if they receive information through social workers, neighbors of recipients, a hotline, or other sources regarding TANF recipients misusing their TANF benefits, they could assign a protective payee to TANF recipients who display misuse of their TANF benefits.[40]

---

[37]1 Tex. Admin. Code §§ 372.1701 - 1702.

[38]According to HHSC officials, TANF-only retailers are those retailers that have the ability to redeem TANF benefits in Texas, but are not authorized by FNS to redeem SNAP benefits.

[39]Tex. Hum. Res. Code § 31.0355(a). Subsequent state regulations expanded the list of permissible purchases to include furniture, laundry, household supplies, and recreation. See 1 Tex. Admin. Code § 372.1509(b).

[40]Texas state regulations define a TANF protective payee as "a person whom HHSC selects to receive and manage benefits for the certified group instead of the caretaker. HHSC may designate a protective payee whenever HHSC determines that the caretaker has failed to comply with one or more program requirements." See 1 Tex. Admin. Code §§ 372.2(17) and 372.905(a).

According to state officials, in May 2012, 84 active TANF cases were assigned a protective payee. In addition, TANF recipients are not able to access their benefits at ATMs in Texas, as the state's EBT cards are not accepted at ATMs there.

Washington

Washington has implemented a system in which retailers are responsible for blocking unauthorized TANF transactions, and will soon employ monitoring efforts to determine the effectiveness of its actions. As of January 1, 2012, businesses falling under one of Washington's nine prohibited categories (see fig. 1 above) are required by Washington law to disable the ability of ATM and POS machines located on their premises to accept the state's EBT card.[41] State-licensed taverns, nightclubs, beer/wine specialty stores, bail bond agencies, gambling establishments, and tattoo, body piercing, or body-art shops can have their state business licenses suspended by various state regulatory agencies if it is determined that they are not in compliance with this Washington law.[42] For example, the Washington State Liquor Control Board is required to suspend the licenses of taverns, beer/wine stores, and nightclubs if they are not in compliance. However, because there are no specific statewide licensing requirements for Washington adult-entertainment establishments or establishments where individuals under the age of 18 are not permitted, it is unclear what penalties might apply to those businesses. According to one official from Washington State Department of Social and Health Services (DSHS), DSHS will rely on businesses to ensure that third-party processors have deactivated the state's BIN from relevant machines in the restricted locations, and businesses will be held accountable if DSHS finds that the third-party processors have failed to perform these deactivations. However, one DSHS official stated that DSHS was able to work with the state's tribal casinos, EBT vendor, liquor control board, and gaming commission to disable EBT access at ATMs in casinos and liquor stores.[43] To do so, according to DSHS officials, the state's EBT vendor contacted tribal casinos and commercial bingo establishments to identify the relevant third-party processors and ATM

---

[41]Wash. Rev. Code § 74.08.580(2).

[42]Wash. Rev. Code §§ 66.24.013, 18.185.056, 9.46.410, and 18.300.095.

[43]By June 1, 2012, all state-run liquor stores were closed, and sale and distribution of liquor in the state was privatized. See Wash. Initiative Measure No. 1183 (Nov. 8, 2011).

owners, and then asked them to deactivate the state's BIN from their machines.

Although Washington law requires that certain retailers disable TANF EBT access at ATMs and POS devices on their premises, a state official said that in order to implement the EBT restrictions, the owners of ATMs and POS terminals must manually disable the state's BIN at the ATMs and POS machines. However, DSHS officials clarified that it is possible for larger businesses to perform this remotely. According to officials from DSHS, some retailers may not be aware of the new state law, especially small "mom and pop" retailers. DSHS has coordinated with state licensing agencies to educate licensees about the new requirements affecting them, according to officials from DSHS. However, according to one DSHS official, there are ways to circumvent the state's laws, such as businesses reactivating the state's BIN or changing the location of an ATM after the business obtained or renewed its license.

One official from DSHS also said that the department monitors EBT transaction data to test whether certain retailers are complying with the requirement to disable EBT access on their premises. However, according to one official, although the EBT transaction data may have address information of a business that may match the address of an ATM transaction, this does not necessarily mean that the ATM is located physically on the business's premises. DSHS officials said that they are still considering, but have not yet decided whether to use undercover investigators with loaded EBT cards to test on-site whether retailers are in compliance.

State officials also said that in the past they faced challenges in identifying and classifying locations pursuant to some definitions of prohibited locations. For example, DSHS officials said that the state's gaming regulations classified a certain game as gambling, in which children use a claw to try to win toys, candy, or other prizes. According to state officials, the regulations were changed so that they would not classify these types of games as gambling. In addition, state officials told us that adult-entertainment establishments are not regulated by the state, which may complicate the monitoring of these retailers' compliance with state law due to the uncertainty about what agencies are actually responsible for these specific retailers. For example, one DSHS official told us that DSHS contacted local law enforcement to ask what adult-entertainment establishments are located in their jurisdictions, in an attempt to identify establishments that should disable their EBT access.

Washington state law allows TANF recipients to use their TANF cash assistance to pay for a reasonable amount of basic living expenses, such as shelter, food, transportation, clothing, household maintenance, personal hygiene, employment or school related items, or other necessary incidentals and items. However, state law prohibits individuals from using their EBT cards or TANF cash assistance for gambling activities or to purchase lottery tickets, tobacco, cigarettes, horse racing, or for the purpose of participating in or purchasing any activities located in nightclubs, adult-entertainment venues, establishments where persons under the age of 18 are not permitted, contract liquor stores, bail bond agencies, beer/wine stores, taverns, gambling establishments, or a licensed tattoo, body piercing, or body art shop (see fig. 1 above).[44] Individuals who violate this provision can be fined, forfeit future cash assistance, or after more than one violation be assigned a protective payee.[45] Under state regulations, violators can also be required to provide proof that the cash assistance is being used for the benefit of the children in the household.[46] DSHS officials also said that they are unable to restrict specific types of purchases. Rather, they would need to either completely disable the state's BIN at affected POS devices or allow everything to be purchased with an EBT card. As a result, DSHS officials told us that they rely on the honor system and hope that retailers will stop individuals from using their EBT cards to purchase prohibited items. One DSHS official told us that it is difficult to track how individuals spend the cash withdrawn with their EBT cards. However, DSHS officials stated that if in the course of working with a TANF client the case managers find that the family is consistently in financial crisis and cannot adequately explain why, the case managers might assume the client is not expending the benefits appropriately or wisely. According to DSHS officials, in those instances, the case managers will delve deeper and talk with the clients to determine if they are using their benefits correctly by meeting the basic needs of the clients' families and assist the clients with understanding how the TANF benefits should be used. If these issues continue, the case managers may suggest or require that a protective payee be assigned.

---

[44]Wash. Rev. Code § 74.08.580(1).

[45]Wash. Rev. Code § 74.08.580(5). Washington state regulation defines a protective payee as "a person or an employee of an agency who manages client cash benefits to provide for basic needs—housing, utilities, clothing, child care, and food." See Wash. Admin. Code § 388-460-0020(1).

[46]Wash. Admin. Code § 388-412-0046(1)(e)(ii).

States without Restrictions	Four of our 10 selected states—Florida, Illinois, New York, and Ohio—do not have any restrictions aimed at preventing certain TANF transactions. This is because they have no state laws, executive orders, or other regulations that prohibit certain TANF transactions on the basis of the location of the transaction or the nature of the goods or services purchased. In addition, these states did not implement restrictions due to concerns about cost effectiveness or technical limitations, according to state officials. As mentioned above, before the recent passage of the Welfare Integrity and Data Improvement Act, as part of the Middle Class Tax Relief and Job Creation Act of 2012, states were not required to maintain or implement policies or practices aimed at preventing certain TANF transactions in certain locations. TANF was designed to provide states with great flexibility in determining how to run their own programs. Although states are required to implement policies and practices aimed at preventing certain TANF transactions in certain locations by February 22, 2014, there is currently no nationwide restriction on how TANF recipients can spend their TANF cash assistance. Because of these factors, these 4 states have not attempted to block or prohibit certain TANF transactions at certain locations or to prohibit the purchase of certain goods and services, unlike the other 6 states discussed above.

Other additional factors also influenced these states' decisions not to restrict certain TANF transactions. For example, officials in Florida and New York told us that they reviewed the number of EBT transactions conducted at certain locations—casinos and liquor stores in Florida; bingo halls, casinos, and off-track betting sites in New York—and compared that number to the total number of EBT transactions. They found that only a small percentage of transactions took place at these locations.[47] Therefore, officials in these states determined that it would not be cost-effective to implement restrictions aimed at preventing a relatively small number of transactions.

New York officials did note later that liquor stores in New York are precluded from having ATMs. In addition, New York officials noted that they received voluntary cooperation, over the last several years, from merchants and ATM providers to prevent TANF transactions initiated with the New York EBT card in select gambling establishments located in New York and other states serviced by these merchants and ATM providers.

---

[47]We did not independently verify the results of these reviews.

New York officials stated that merchants have accomplished this by identifying TANF transactions initiated at ATMs in select gambling establishments and declining such transactions that are associated with New York's BIN for EBT transactions. New York officials noted this methodology as one possible cost-effective way to prevent electronic transactions with TANF funds at certain locations because it would entail that the merchants direct their third-party processor to block the states' EBT cards' BINs from being able to complete an ATM or POS transaction in certain establishments. According to New York officials, third-party processors can add and block BINs regularly through software updates. According to New York officials, this can be done as part of the service third-party processors provide to business establishments through their service agreements, which could be performed at no extra cost to the business establishments.

Illinois officials told us that their current EBT contract did not include the capability to block certain locations from EBT access. Although Illinois officials said that their state had no restrictions in place to block certain TANF transactions, they said that state casinos voluntarily disabled EBT access at ATMs on their premises—this is similar to the voluntary efforts by casinos in Michigan and Pennsylvania. Ohio is unique among our 10 selected states in that it uses EPC cards to distribute TANF cash assistance rather than EBT cards. State officials told us that they chose to use EPC cards because of the increased accessibility they provide to recipients. Because federal financial-privacy laws generally prevent the state from receiving data on individual EPC transactions, unless a specified exception exists,[48] state officials said that they are unable to monitor or restrict the use of EPC cards at certain locations.

States May Face Challenges in Implementing Restrictions

States may face challenges in implementing future restrictions on TANF transactions. As mentioned above, the Welfare Integrity and Data Improvement Act, part of the Middle Class Tax Relief and Job Creation Act of 2012, will require states to prevent TANF electronic benefit transactions at certain locations.[49] In addition, the law requires that HHS

---

[48]12 U.S.C. § 3402.

[49]As stated above, states will be required to have in place policies and practices as necessary to prevent such transactions within 2 years of the Act's enactment. Pub. L. No. 112–96, § 4004(b), 126 Stat. 156, 197–198.

determine whether states have implemented and maintained such policies and practices for preventing these transactions. At the time of this report's issuance, HHS was at the beginning of its rulemaking process and it did not yet know what form its final regulations would take. As such, it was too early to determine what states will need to do in order to comply with the new federal requirements. Officials from multiple states told us that the federal requirements are expected to help states ensure that cash assistance is used in a manner reflecting the purpose of TANF. However, some officials cited challenges that they might face in attempting to prevent certain TANF transactions in order to meet the potential requirements of the law. These challenges were primarily focused on difficulties with identifying locations that could be blocked from EBT access and limitations in available data. For example, according to officials from multiple states, the transaction data they receive do not contain information that is accurate or detailed enough for them to identify locations that could potentially be prohibited or restricted. If transaction data are inaccurate or lack enough information about the business nature of specific retailers, states' efforts to prevent certain TANF transactions may be impeded. State officials suggested that improvements in the quality of EBT transaction data might better enable them to prevent such transactions. For example, state officials suggested that prevention efforts would be aided by more-accurate and complete address information for transactions, or requiring merchant category codes to be included in the data. In addition, officials from multiple states suggested that businesses or third-party processors should be responsible for ensuring that EBT access is disabled at certain locations, rather than states.

We found that EBT transaction data from four states—California, Florida, New York, and Texas—contained incomplete or inaccurate information for the address of the location where the transaction occurred, which limits the data's usefulness for systematic monitoring.[50] To conduct systematic monitoring effectively, including the identification of locations that can be blocked from EBT access, data should be complete and accurate. In the California and Florida data, the address information was sufficiently complete; however, it was not sufficiently accurate. We estimate that the reported addresses of the locations where the transactions occurred could be linked to standardized addresses for less

---

[50]As mentioned above, we assessed EBT data from these four states containing transactions made from October 1, 2009, through September 30, 2010.

than 21 percent and 14 percent of the transactions, respectively.[51] This means that the states could not rely on the majority of the transaction records for accurately identifying a true location and would therefore need to verify manually that the reported addresses for the transactions matched to a real location, which would increase the time and labor required as part of this process. The New York EBT data contained complete address information for approximately 71 percent of the transactions, of which we estimate that up to 34.2 percent could be linked to standardized addresses.[52]

Texas address information was complete for approximately 30 percent of the transactions,[53] although we estimate that as many as 70.4 percent of those addresses could be linked to standardized addresses. Without sufficiently complete and accurate information for the address where an EBT transaction occurred, states are unable to systematically monitor or block EBT access. To the extent that the information is available, states could use EBT data to identify individual transactions that may have occurred at certain locations on the basis of the name of the merchant at the location where the transaction occurred. We found that the merchant name was available for approximately 19 million transactions—45 percent of the transactions we examined—as low as 30 percent in Texas and as high as 90 percent in Florida.

Officials from multiple states and representatives from states' EBT vendors expressed concerns about the EBT data. For example, according to one vendor, address information in the data— which is self-reported by ATM or POS device owners or operators, and is transmitted by third-party processors—is not always correct, and the ATM addresses listed in the data sometimes do not reflect where transactions actually took place. In addition, state officials and representatives from states' EBT vendors stated that the ATM transaction data maintained by vendors all list the same merchant category code that provides no information about the type

---

[51]As mentioned above, we compared EBT transaction addresses to U.S. Census Bureau TIGER standard addresses. Estimates include a margin of error of no more than 3.3 percent for California and 2.8 percent for Florida at the 95 percent confidence level.

[52]Estimate includes a margin of error of no more than 4.1 percent at the 95 percent confidence level.

[53]Estimate includes a margin of error of no more than 4.2 percent at the 95 percent confidence level.

of retailer where the ATM machines are located. According to state and vendor officials, the inaccuracies and insufficiencies in the EBT transaction data are due to gaps in data reporting and the nature of the EBT system's infrastructure. According to representatives from one EBT vendor, third-party processors do not always verify the information contained in transaction data, which diminishes the quality of the data that they submit to the EBT vendors. According to some state and vendor officials, the EBT transaction data are not used generally for only identifying where TANF transactions might occur.

The EBT program was devised in the 1980s to originally meet the needs of the USDA's Food Stamp Program, in which federal benefits would be disbursed electronically to eligible recipients, with states later adding their TANF programs to EBT cards. Some state officials and vendor representatives noted that the specifications governing the extent of the EBT data captured as part of an EBT transaction do not require all transaction information on each EBT transaction.[54] For example, according to state officials from Texas, some data elements, such as merchant names, could be useful for monitoring where TANF benefits are accessed, but they are not required under those specifications. The accuracy of the data is also affected by self-reporting. For example, although it is intended that the transactions follow these specifications, key industry players, such as third-party processors, do not follow these specifications consistently, according to California officials. Moreover, because transactions can go through multiple entities, including third-party processors, the transaction data can change and may not always be transmitted accurately to the vendor, according to California officials.

As mentioned above, Ohio is unique among our selected 10 states in disbursing TANF cash assistance through EPC cards rather than EBT cards. Regarding potential future restrictions, Ohio officials told us that they are unsure how they will be able to restrict TANF transactions, and will need to work with their vendor that operates their EPC state card to determine the feasibility of performing these restrictions. However, according to one vendor, given that EPC cards are branded by major financial institutions—such as Visa and MasterCard—and operate on

---

[54]These state officials and vendor representatives said that EBT transactions follow ISO 8583, which is the International Standard designed as an interface specification enabling messages relating to financial transactions to be exchanged between systems adopting a variety of application specifications.

these institutions' commercial infrastructure, these institutions could disable POS access for EPC cards by using merchant category codes that retailers are required to submit as part of the transaction data in order to participate in the institutions' networks. This type of blocking is not possible, however, with ATMs that accept EPC cards, according to representatives from one vendor. However, vendor representatives told us that ATM data for EPC transactions, similar to EBT card data, contain only one merchant category code for all terminals, identifying the location of the transaction as a financial institution. Also similar to EBT card data, EPC card data do not contain detailed information on items purchased with the EPC cards.

Concluding Observations

The purpose of TANF is to help needy families achieve self-sufficiency. Providing TANF benefits by means of electronic benefit cards helps the banked and unbanked TANF recipients, gives TANF recipients an alternate to cash, and allows states to use existing infrastructures. However, any misuse of TANF funds not only deprives low-income families of needed assistance, but also diminishes public trust in both the integrity of the program and the federal government. Before Congress passed the Welfare Integrity and Data Improvement Act, as part of the Middle Class Tax Relief and Job Creation Act of 2012, some states acted independently to implement restrictions on certain TANF transactions. As a result, their approach to enacting restrictions varies significantly. However, until HHS issues regulations or provides further guidance as to what policies and practices are sufficient to comply with the new federal requirements, it is unclear to what extent the various restrictions implemented by states would be in compliance. The experience of these states—especially any information related to the cost-effectiveness and success rates for various restrictions—could be beneficial for HHS to consider as it works toward determining what policies and practices are sufficient to comply with the new federal law. As we heard from officials in multiple states, preventing unauthorized transactions can be time-intensive and is impaired by flaws in available transaction data and other challenges. Addressing the limitations we found in transaction data that impede the identification and monitoring of certain locations could require significant resources. Therefore, restriction methods that do not rely on flawed transaction data may be the most practical, such as Washington state's requirement for businesses to independently disable EBT access or risk losing or not obtaining their state licenses to operate.

Agency and State Comments

We provided a draft of this report to HHS for comment. In its written comments, reproduced in appendix III, HHS noted that our report highlights many of the challenges and issues states and others face in issuing the TANF requirements that Congress enacted in February 2012. In addition, HHS stated that our report's findings and analysis will be helpful as HHS drafts implementing regulations relevant to these TANF requirements. HHS also provided technical comments that we incorporated, as appropriate.

In May 2012, we also provided the 10 selected states with an opportunity to comment on our draft findings relevant to their specific TANF programs. In May 2012, 7 of the 10 selected states provided us with technical comments by e-mail, and we incorporated their technical comments as appropriate. Three states, Illinois, Massachusetts, and Pennsylvania, had no comments.

As agreed with your office, unless you publicly announce the contents of this report earlier, we plan no further distribution until 7 days from the report date. At that time, we will send copies to other interested congressional committees and the Secretary of Health and Human Services. In addition, the report will be available at no charge on the GAO website at http://www.gao.gov.

If you or your staff have any questions about this report, please contact me at (202) 512-6722 or kutzg@gao.gov. Contact points for our Offices of Congressional Relations and Public Affairs may be found on the last page of this report. GAO staff who made key contributions to this report are listed in appendix IV.

Sincerely yours,

Gregory D. Kutz
Director, Forensic Audits and Investigative Service

Appendix I: Objectives, Scope, and Methodology

Our objective was to determine the extent to which selected states have taken action to prevent unauthorized Temporary Assistance for Needy Families (TANF) transactions. To conduct our work, we reviewed TANF laws, regulations, and other documentation—including the Welfare Integrity and Data Improvement Act, part of the Middle Class Tax Relief and Job Creation Act of 2012, which introduced new state requirements for preventing certain TANF transactions—and interviewed officials from Health and Human Services (HHS). From each selected state, we reviewed information related to its laws, policies, practices, and other factors affecting its TANF program. In addition, we interviewed and reviewed documentation from several key industry stakeholders related to states' efforts to prevent unauthorized TANF transactions. We also interviewed officials from the top 10 states in terms of TANF basic block-grant dollars—California, New York, Michigan, Ohio, Pennsylvania, Illinois, Florida, Texas, Massachusetts, and Washington. Together, these 10 states represent a total of 66 percent of TANF basic block-grant funds.[1] The industry stakeholders included: JP Morgan Chase and Affiliated Computer Services, the two largest vendors providing TANF electronic benefit card services to the states; the Electronic Funds Transfer Association, an industry trade association that conducts work related to electronic benefit card services for government agencies at the federal and state level; the National Conference of State Legislatures, a bipartisan organization that provides research and other services to state legislators and their staff; and the American Public Human Services Association, a bipartisan, nonprofit organization representing appointed state and local health and human-services agency commissioners. We obtained electronic benefit card transaction data from 4 of the 10 selected states—California, Florida, New York, and Texas—covering transactions from federal fiscal year 2010.[2] We selected these 4 states based on geographical diversity. The results of our analysis of these 4 states' data cannot be generalized to other states.[3] Using these data, we assessed

---

[1]California represents 22.6 percent of total national TANF basic block grant dollars; New York, 14.8 percent; Michigan, 4.7 percent; Ohio, 4.4 percent; Pennsylvania, 4.4 percent; Illinois, 3.5 percent; Florida, 3.4 percent; Texas, 2.9 percent; Massachusetts, 2.8 percent; and Washington, 2.5 percent in fiscal year 2012.

[2]October 1, 2009, to September 30, 2010.

[3]The random samples can only generalize about each state using each state's sample, not about other states and not nationally. For example, the Texas sample tells us something general about the Texas EBT data as a whole, but cannot tell us anything about the California data or all U.S. data.

the extent to which the data would allow the 4 selected states to conduct systematic monitoring of TANF transactions. Such monitoring might include an assessment of the prevalence of transactions at certain locations.

To do so, we used a generalizable, random sample of each of the 4 selected states' Electronic Benefit Transfer (EBT) transaction data and compared it to electronic geo-coding information that pinpoints places and identifies locations.[4] Subsequent visual inspection and manual cleaning of obvious address errors in the EBT data only resulted in a small portion of corrected location addresses. We also assessed whether the data would allow states to identify individual TANF transactions at certain types of locations. To do so, we conducted keyword searches of merchant names for terms that are potentially associated with casinos, liquor stores, and adult-entertainment establishments. We performed data checks to determine the reliability of the California, Florida, New York, and Texas EBT data for the purposes of our engagement. For all four states, we determined that the EBT data are not sufficiently reliable for the purpose of performing systematic monitoring, as the selected states' data contained incomplete or inaccurate information for the addresses of the locations where the transactions occurred. Given the combination of both completeness and accuracy issues in the 4 selected states, we also determined most of the data in the 4 selected states could not match to address location information that would allow for suitable comparisons to other potential data sources. However, we determined that the transaction data would support keyword searches of merchant names for terms that are associated potentially with casinos, liquor stores, and adult-entertainment establishments, for records that contain merchant names. We conducted this performance audit from October 2012 to July 2012, in accordance with generally accepted government auditing standards. Those standards require that we plan and perform the audit to obtain sufficient, appropriate evidence to provide a reasonable basis for our findings and conclusions based on our audit objectives. We believe that the evidence obtained provides a reasonable basis for our findings and conclusions based on our audit objectives.

---

[4]We compared EBT transaction addresses to U.S. Census Bureau's Topologically Integrated Geographic Encoding and Referencing (TIGER) standard addresses.

The table below includes figure 1's (see above) rollover information and describes the steps that 6 of the 10 states we reviewed have taken that are aimed at preventing the use Temporary Assistance for Needy Families (TANF) cash assistance for certain purchases or in certain locations.

Table 1: Some States Have Taken Steps Aimed at Preventing Unauthorized TANF Transactions

State	Steps taken
California	- EBT access disabled at ATMs in California businesses, including - Casinos - Adult-entertainment businesses - Bail-bond locations - Night clubs/saloons/taverns - Bingo halls - Race tracks - Gun/ammunition stores - Cruise ships - Psychic readers - Smoking shops - Cannabis shops - Tattoo/piercing shops - Spa/massage salons - Liquor stores not authorized by the Food and Nutrition Service (FNS)
Massachusetts	- TANF recipients in Massachusetts are prohibited by state law from using cash assistance to purchase - Alcohol - Tobacco - Lottery tickets - Merchants in Massachusetts are prohibited by state law from knowingly accepting EBT cards for the purchase of - Alcoholic beverages - Tobacco products - Lottery tickets
Michigan	- TANF recipients in Michigan are prohibited by state law and policies from using their TANF cash assistance for - Lottery tickets - Alcohol - Tobacco - Gambling - Illegal activities, including purchasing illegal drugs - Adult entertainment - Massage parlors - Spas - Tattoo shops - Bail-bond agencies - Cruise ships - Nonessential items, including items not necessary to sustain the household - EBT access disabled at ATMs in Michigan casinos

State	Steps taken
Pennsylvania	- No ATMs exist in Pennsylvania-run liquor stores[a]
	- Pennsylvania liquor stores do not accept Pennsylvania's EBT card at POS terminals
	- EBT access disabled at ATMs in licensed casinos in Pennsylvania
	- By Pennsylvania law, TANF cash assistance shall be diminished by amounts that a Pennsylvania TANF recipient obtains by cashing a TANF cash assistance check at a Pennsylvania gambling casino, racetrack, bingo hall or other establishment which derives more than 50 percent of its gross revenue from gambling
	- TANF recipients are prohibited from using their EBT card to purchase liquor or alcohol

Washington	- Washington merchants are required by state law to disable ATMs and POS terminals located in their
	  - Casinos
	  - Liquor stores
	  - Taverns
	  - Nightclubs
	  - Bail-bond agencies
	  - Body-art shops
	  - Race tracks
	  - Adult-entertainment venues
	  - Establishments where persons under the age of 18 are not permitted

	- Washington TANF recipients are prohibited by state law from using TANF cash assistance for
	  - Gambling
	  - Amusement games
	  - Raffling
	  - Horse racing
	  - Lottery tickets
	  - Cigarettes
	  - Tobacco products
	  - Body piercings
	  - Beer
	  - Wine
	  - Adult-entertainment materials
	  - Bail bonds

Texas	- TANF recipients in Texas are not able to access their TANF cash assistance at ATMs[a]

	- Retailers participating in the Texas EBT program must be either FNS-authorized or nonfood retailers that receive no more than 10 percent of their gross revenue from entertainment, such as from the sale of
	  - Alcoholic beverages
	  - Legalized games of chance
	  - Sexually oriented materials
	  - Coin-operated amusement machines or amusement services

	- TANF recipients in Texas can only use their TANF cash assistance for goods and services necessary and essential to the welfare of the family

Source: GAO.

[a]Liquor stores in Pennsylvania are operated by the state.

[b]TANF recipients in Texas can use their EBT cards to make purchases of approved items or take out cash at participating retailers' POS devices

Appendix III: Comments from the Department of Health and Human Services

DEPARTMENT OF HEALTH & HUMAN SERVICES

OFFICE OF THE SECRETARY

Assistant Secretary for Legislation
Washington, DC 20201

JUN 27 2012

Greg Kutz, Director
Forensic Audits and Investigative Service
U.S. Government Accountability Office
441 G Street NW
Washington, DC 20548

Dear Mr. Kutz

Attached are comments on the U.S. Government Accountability Office's (GAO) report entitled:
"TANF-ELECTRONIC BENEFIT CARDS: Some States Are Restricting Certain TANF
Transactions, but Challenges Remain" (GAO-12-535).

The Department appreciates the opportunity to review this draft section of the report prior to
publication.

Sincerely,

Jim R. Esquea
Assistant Secretary for Legislation

Attachment

**GENERAL COMMENTS OF THE DEPARTMENT OF HEALTH AND HUMAN
SERVICES (HHS) ON THE GOVERNMENT ACCOUNTABILITY OFFICE'S (GAO)
DRAFT REPORT ENTITLED, "TANF-ELECTRONIC BENEFIT CARDS: SOME
STATES ARE RESTRICTING CERTAIN TANF TRANSACTIONS, BUT
CHALLENGES REMAIN" (GAO-12-535)**

The Department appreciates the opportunity to comment on this draft report.

HHS appreciates the information and analysis provided in GAO's review of the experiences of
ten states relating to restricting electronic benefits transactions in certain locations or for certain
purposes. As the report explains, Congress has directed states to develop and maintain policies
and practices to prevent Temporary Assistance for Needy Families (TANF) cash assistance from
being used in any electronic benefit transfer transaction in liquor stores; casinos, gambling
casinos or gaming establishments; or any retail establishment which provides adult-oriented
entertainment in which performers disrobe or perform in an unclothed state for entertainment.
As the report also notes, HHS has solicited comments from states, businesses, consumer
advocates, and any other interested persons so that HHS can draw from the states' experiences as
HHS drafts regulations to implement the statutory provision.

The report highlights the many challenges and issues that are faced in any effort to implement
such a requirement. GAO's information and analysis will be helpful as HHS drafts its
implementing regulations.

1

Appendix IV: GAO Contact and Staff Acknowledgments

GAO Contact	Gregory D. Kutz, (202) 512-6722 or kutzg@gao.gov
Staff Acknowledgments	In addition to the contact named above, Cindy Brown Barnes, Assistant Director; Erika Axelson, Assistant Director; Christopher W. Backley; Melinda Cordero; Justin Fisher; Katherine Forsyth; Gale Harris; Olivia Lopez; Grant Mallie; Flavio J. Martinez; Maria McMullen; James Murphy; Anna Maria Ortiz; Robert C. Rodgers; Rebecca Shea; and Timothy Walker made key contributions to this report.

GAO's Mission	The Government Accountability Office, the audit, evaluation, and investigative arm of Congress, exists to support Congress in meeting its constitutional responsibilities and to help improve the performance and accountability of the federal government for the American people. GAO examines the use of public funds; evaluates federal programs and policies; and provides analyses, recommendations, and other assistance to help Congress make informed oversight, policy, and funding decisions. GAO's commitment to good government is reflected in its core values of accountability, integrity, and reliability.
Obtaining Copies of GAO Reports and Testimony	The fastest and easiest way to obtain copies of GAO documents at no cost is through GAO's website (www.gao.gov). Each weekday afternoon, GAO posts on its website newly released reports, testimony, and correspondence. To have GAO e-mail you a list of newly posted products, go to www.gao.gov and select "E-mail Updates."
Order by Phone	The price of each GAO publication reflects GAO's actual cost of production and distribution and depends on the number of pages in the publication and whether the publication is printed in color or black and white. Pricing and ordering information is posted on GAO's website, http://www.gao.gov/ordering.htm.

Place orders by calling (202) 512-6000, toll free (866) 801-7077, or TDD (202) 512-2537.

Orders may be paid for using American Express, Discover Card, MasterCard, Visa, check, or money order. Call for additional information. |
| **Connect with GAO** | Connect with GAO on Facebook, Flickr, Twitter, and YouTube. Subscribe to our RSS Feeds or E-mail Updates. Listen to our Podcasts. Visit GAO on the web at www.gao.gov. |
| **To Report Fraud, Waste, and Abuse in Federal Programs** | Contact:

Website: www.gao.gov/fraudnet/fraudnet.htm
E-mail: fraudnet@gao.gov
Automated answering system: (800) 424-5454 or (202) 512-7470 |
| **Congressional Relations** | Katherine Siggerud, Managing Director, siggerudk@gao.gov, (202) 512-4400, U.S. Government Accountability Office, 441 G Street NW, Room 7125, Washington, DC 20548 |
| **Public Affairs** | Chuck Young, Managing Director, youngc1@gao.gov, (202) 512-4800 U.S. Government Accountability Office, 441 G Street NW, Room 7149 Washington, DC 20548 |

Please Print on Recycled Paper.

www.ingramcontent.com/pod-product-compliance
Lightning Source LLC
Chambersburg PA
CBHW080930290526
45795CB00007BA/2692